Natural Trimmings

Christmas Customs

Natural Trimmings

CREATIVE
PUBLISHING
international

MINNETONKA, MINNESOTA

President/CEO: David D. Murphy

CHRISTMAS CUSTOMS: NATURAL TRIMMINGS
Created by the editors of Creative Publishing international.

Executive Editor: Elaine Perry
Senior Editor: Linda Neubauer
Senior Art Director: Stephanie Michaud
Art Director: Mark Jacobson
Desktop Publishing Specialist: Laurie Kristensen
Project & Prop Stylist: Joanne Wawra
Samplemaker: Arlene Dohrman
Photographer: Tate Carlson
Director of Production Services: Kim Gerber

Creative Publishing international, Inc. offers a variety of how-to
books. For information write:
   Creative Publishing international, Inc.
      Subscriber Books
   5900 Green Oak Drive
   Minnetonka, MN 55343

ISBN 1-58923-013-2

Printed in Singapore
10 9 8 7 6 5 4 3 2 1

Table of Contents

The fresh scent of pine, the colorful and fragrant display of fruits and flowers, and the distinctive forms of pinecones, seashells, and holly are some of Mother Nature's contributions to the Christmas season. For centuries these commonplace things have been brought inside to decorate our homes and instill holiday spirit, for in their simplicity we find beauty and promise. Many of the traditions of decorating with these natural trimmings have ancient origins, some dating to a time before Christmas celebrations began. In telling of their folklore and legends, this book intends to give more significance to holiday decorating and to attribute more purpose to the customary decking of the halls.

Evergreen Boughs

In the cold, dark winter, when it seems all other plants have died, evergreens keep their fresh green color and remain alive. No wonder in ancient times, people revered the evergreen trees and attributed mystical powers to them. The evergreen tree became a symbol of life that promised hope for the coming spring. In medieval times, people used the leaves and needles of bay, fir, ivy, juniper, larch, pine, spruce, and yew to adorn houses and stables in winter, believing their powers would protect the families and their animals. The mystical aura of evergreen branches found its way into early Christmas traditions as well, when people hung greenery in their windows to ward off evil spirits. It was believed that a witch would not enter a home that had been decorated with evergreen boughs until she had counted every needle! Today the magic powers of the evergreen tree are all but forgotten, yet evergreen boughs remain at the heart of our Christmas decorating, with their fresh pine scent and lush green color.

How to make a Fresh Garland

Materials

- Fresh greens.
- Lightweight rope or twine.
- 22-gauge paddle floral wire or chenille stems.
- Pruning shears.
- Wire cutter.

1 Tie rope to solid overhead object, such as ceiling-mounted plant hook. Cut fresh greens into sprigs. Wire three sprigs to rope, with tips facing up, placing two in front and one in back; wrap wire at the base of the sprigs.

2 Continue wiring greens around rope, overlapping them to conceal the wire. At desired length, wire full tips of greens to bottom of garland, concealing ends of sprigs.

3 Cut the wire and rope at ends of garland; knot ends, forming loops for hanging, if desired.

1

2

3

Holly sprigs are incorporated into the pine garland for a contrast in texture and a splash of color. Decorative cords and tassels enrich the look, and twinkling lights add to the festivity. To protect wood surfaces, use wrapped floral wire when making the garland and attach it to the banister with chenille stems or ribbons.

Garland is used traditionally to dress the mantel. To secure the garland without nailing into the mantel itself, cut a 1 × 1 board the length of the mantel. Stain or paint the board to match the mantel, and pound nails into the board for securing the garland.

Bow-shaped garland is hung over the fireplace instead of a wreath. Tie a wide ribbon to the ends of the garland, and hang the garland from the ribbon.

How to make a
Fresh Evergreen Spray Centerpiece

Fresh evergreen sprays, placed end-to-end and topped with a bow, make a quick and attractive centerpiece. Candles are nestled in the greens.

Materials

- Fresh tips from various evergreens; cedar greens work well for the base.
- 22-gauge or 24-gauge wire; wire cutter; floral tape.
- Embellishments as desired, such as candles, ribbon, and berries.

1 Layer fresh greens, and secure stems with wire. Wrap wired stems with floral tape to protect the table, stretching the tape as it is applied. Repeat to make two garlands.

2 Overlap and wire stems of layered greens together; cover with floral tape.

3 Make bow with long streamers, and secure to greens, concealing wired stems. Twist and loop the streamers among the greens. Arrange candles and other embellishments as desired.

1

2

3

How to make a Tabletop Evergreen Tree

Preserved evergreens, such as spruce, cedar, or boxwood are used to make this ever-fresh tabletop tree. Carefully stored, it will last from year to year. Preserved natural greens can be purchased from florists or floral crafting centers.

Materials

- Styrofoam® cone, about 18" (46 cm) high with 5" (12.5 cm) base.
- Woven basket with 5" (12.5 cm) base.
- Spanish moss.
- Preserved or artificial greens, such as spruce, cedar, and boxwood.
- 20 or more pinecones in various sizes.
- 11 yd. (10.1 m) ribbon, 3/8" (1 cm) wide.
- Several stems of small berries.
- Dried naturals, such as statice or baby's breath.
- 3" (7.5 cm) wooden floral picks with wire.
- Pruning shears; wire cutter.
- Craft glue; hot glue gun and glue sticks.

1

2

1 Apply hot glue to the top of the inverted basket; secure cone to basket. Arrange Spanish moss on cone, pulling moss apart so it loosely covers Styrofoam; secure with dots of hot glue, using glue sparingly.

2 Cut greens into sprigs ranging from 3" to 6" (7.5 to 15 cm) long, making angled cuts. Insert the stems into cone, angling the sprigs so they point downward; place longer sprigs at the bottom of the cone and shorter ones toward the top.

3 Cut boxwood into pieces ranging from 3" to 6" (7.5 to 15 cm) long; intersperse other greens with boxwood.

4 Wire pinecones to wooden picks. Insert pinecones, placing larger ones at the bottom and smaller ones at the top.

5 Cut berries into about 20 clusters; wire them to picks, and arrange on cone. Or attach stemmed clusters by inserting stems directly into cone.

6 Cut 15 to 20 clusters of statice; wire them to picks. Insert picks into cone, angling clusters so they point downward.

7 Cut ribbon into 1-yd. (0.95 m) lengths. Fold ribbon, forming three or four loops on each side; leave two tails, with one tail about 2" (5 cm) longer than the other. Attach to a wooden pick with wire, wrapping the wire around the center of the bow several times.

8 Wrap longer tail of bow twice around center, concealing the wire; secure with the remaining wire, and twist wire around pick.

9 Attach bows to cone tree, inserting picks. Attach one bow to the top of the tree; shorten the pick on this bow, if necessary, and secure with glue.

4

5

6

7

Natural Wreaths

Wreaths made of evergreens are a mainstay of the Christmas season. While decorating nearly every door on the street, wreaths also are seen hanging from light poles, gates, and even over the front grillwork of a passing car. The wreath's symbolism is derived from its shape and its content. Since ancient times, the circle has been used to represent eternity–it has no beginning and no end–like the cycle of the seasons. Though the earth seemed to die in the cold, dark, days of winter, there was always rebirth and rejuvenation in the spring. As time passed, the wreath came to symbolize victory over life's challenges. The Romans awarded a wreath to the winner of a sporting event as a symbol of victory. Christians later adopted the wreath to represent the eternal nature of God's love and Christ's victory over death. Made of evergreens, the Christmas wreath also symbolizes immortality and faith.

How to make a Fresh Evergreen Wreath

Nothing echoes a Christmas tradition more than wreaths. You can make your own from fresh greens. Or purchase ready-made wreaths and add your own embellishments. Fresh evergreen and eucalyptus wreaths, both easy to make, add fragrance to a room. Other wreath styles, including grapevine and twig wreaths, are available at craft and floral stores.

You may choose to embellish an entire wreath, use a third of the wreath as the design area, or add a single embellishment. It is usually more attractive if the focal point of the design is slightly offset.

Choose embellishments that are in scale with the size of the wreath, and vary the size of the embellishments so there will be a dominant focal point, with smaller items that complement it. Choose items that are harmonious in style, yet provide some contrast in color and texture. Some tips and ideas for embellishing wreaths are shown on pages 22 and 23.

Materials

- Fresh greens.
- 22-gauge or 24-gauge paddle floral wire; wire cutter; pruning shears.
- Coat hanger.
- Ribbon and embellishments as desired.

1 Shape coat hanger into circle. Cut greens into sprigs. Wire three sprigs to hanger, with tips facing up, placing two in front and one in back; wrap wire at base of sprigs.

2 Continue wrapping clusters of greens with wire, overlapping each cluster to conceal wire. When coat hanger is covered, cut some full tips of greens and wire them to hanger, concealing ends of sprigs.

1

2

20

How to make a Eucalyptus Wreath

Materials

- Ready-made straw wreath.
- Eucalyptus with fine stems; two or three bunches will be sufficient for most wreath sizes.
- 22-gauge or 24-gauge paddle floral wire; wire cutter; pruning shears.
- Ribbon and embellishments as desired.

1 Cut eucalyptus in half or in thirds, so each sprig is 6" to 7" (15 to 18 cm) long. Secure the bottom 1" (2.5 cm) of several sprigs to wreath with wire, wrapping the wire around wreath; cover front and sides of wreath.

2 Continue adding sprigs to front and sides of wreath; layer sprigs and wrap with wire, working in one direction. Stagger the length of the tips randomly.

3 Lift tips of sprigs at starting point, and secure last layer of sprigs under them. Make a wire loop for hanging; secure loop to back of the wreath. Embellish as desired.

1

2

3

Tips for Embellishing Wreaths

Separate bunches of dried flowers by holding them over steam for 1 to 2 minutes; remove from steam and pull stems apart gently.

Create a base for anchoring embellishments by wiring a piece of floral foam, which has been covered with moss, to the wreath. Attach embellishments to moss-covered base.

Attach wire to pinecone by wrapping wire around bottom layers of pinecone. Add luster to pinecones by applying glossy brown aerosol paint.

Make picks by grouping items together. Attach wire to items as necessary. Wrap stems and wires with floral tape.

*M*ore Ideas for *Wreaths*

Dried naturals (above, left) are the primary embellishments for this ready-made twig wreath. The bird's nest, slightly off-center on the wreath, becomes the focal point.

Evergreen bouquet (above) of mixed greens and pinecones is wired asymmetrically onto a ready-made grapevine wreath for a quick embellishment. The narrow French ribbon is wrapped loosely around the wreath.

Apples and popcorn (left) are used as the dominant embellishments for this fresh wreath of mixed greens. To carry out the natural look, nuts and pinecones are also used.

Fresh Advent Wreath

There has been much scholarly debate over the actual date on which to celebrate Jesus's birth. The earliest reference to Christmas being celebrated on December 25 appears in Antioch in the second century, at a time when Christians were still persecuted. Two hundred years later, Roman emperor Constantine, who embraced Christianity, made it official. Such a momentous celebration called for a period of preparation, so in 567, the Council of Tours established the period of Advent as a time of fasting before Christmas. Today Advent is recognized as a period of hope and anticipation, beginning four Sundays before Christmas.

To mark this pre-Christmas season, the lighting of the Advent wreath, a custom that originated in eastern Germany, is observed in many homes and churches. Full of symbolism, the wreath is a reminder of many Christian beliefs. The wreath is round as a symbol of eternity. It is made of evergreens to symbolize hope and everlasting life. Four candles, one to be lit each Sunday of Advent, are placed amid the circle of greens. The first candle represents joy, the second hope, the third faith, and the fourth peace. Some choose to add a fifth white candle in the center of the wreath to light on Christmas Day.

How to make a Fresh Advent Wreath

Materials

- 12" (30.5 cm) foam wreath form for fresh flowers.
- Sheet moss; floral pins.
- Four spiked candle cups.
- Assorted greens, 4" to 6" (10 to 15 cm) long.
- Spray bottle and commercial plant protector or floral preservative, optional.
- 1 yd. (0.95 m) ribbon.
- Four or five candles.

1 Soak foam wreath form in water until saturated; dampen the sheet moss. Cover wreath form with sheet moss; secure with floral pins.

2 Insert candle cups into foam, spacing them evenly. Push greens into foam, starting with longest needles and distributing evenly; cut small opening in moss with knife, if necessary. Secure long branch tips with floral pins.

3 Insert any floral stems into foam, spacing them evenly. Mist wreath with water. Wind ribbon through greens. Insert candles into candle cups.

1

2

3

26

$\mathcal{T}$ips for a Longer-Lasting Arrangement

Place wreath on drainboard, and pour at least 1 cup (250 mL) water into foam, as if watering a houseplant. Allow water to soak in.

Cut sprigs of greenery to lengths of 5" to 8" (12.5 to 20.5 cm); trim away any needles near the ends of the sprigs.

Pinecones

An ancient story is told of Mary and Joseph fleeing Herod's soldiers with the baby Jesus. Late one evening, when Mary was too tired to go on, the family took refuge under the branches of a gnarled old pine tree. Hidden from view and sheltered from the elements, they rested for the night while the soldiers passed by unaware. The next morning, feeling safe and rested, they set out again on their journey. But before leaving, the Christ Child blessed the pine tree and left the imprint of his tiny hand forever in the tree's fruit. Cut a fresh pinecone in half lengthwise, and you will see this age-old symbol. Thus, the pinecone has become a classic token of the Christmas season.

How to make a
Single Pinecone Ornament

1 Wrap pine garland around base of cone; secure with hot glue. Embellish garland with berries.

2 Secure bird to top of leaf. Secure leaf to pinecone just above garland.

3 Tie raffia or ribbon around tip of pinecone; then tie in loop for hanger.

2

Materials

- Pinecone.
- Artificial pine garland and berries.
- Hot glue gun and glue sticks.
- Small craft bird.
- Artificial leaf.
- Raffia or ribbon, for hanger.

Pinecones of all shapes and sizes
are used in Christmas decorations
throughout the home. They can be
be used in their natural state, gilded
for an elegant look, or tipped with
white paint to resemble snow.
Here a classic centerpiece is made
from a dried grapevine wreath,
an artificial vine of grape
leaves, dried artichokes,
and gilded pinecones.

Santa pinecone ornaments are quick and inexpensive.
Secure strings for the hangers, using a drop of hot
glue. Form the face, beard, and hairline, using
artificial snow paste; then paint the ornament,
using acrylic paints. Trim the top of the completed
ornament with snow paste.

Pinecones, canella berries, and cedar sprigs combine
to make a fitting natural accent for a package that is
wrapped in brown paper and tied with jute.

Holly

Decking the halls with boughs of holly is a merry Christmas tradition that has its origins in Roman mythology. Because holly stayed green to beautify the forest when the oak trees lost their leaves, the plant took on mystical powers. Ancient Romans wore holly in their hair and decorated images of Saturn, the god of agriculture, during the cold winter months to coax the return of spring. Centuries later, while pagans continued to worship Saturn, early Christians decorated their homes with holly to avoid persecution while secretly celebrating the birth of Jesus. Eventually, this plant, with its shiny green leaves and bright red berries, became a symbol of the peace and joy of Christmas.

Flowers & Fruits

Christmas folklore describes that on the first Noël, the world came to life in miraculous ways: trees bloomed with blossoms and gave fruit although it was winter, animals spoke to each other, and rivers turned to wine. As a result, many early Christmas trees were hung with flowers and fruit to represent the new life that had come into the world. Signs of life in the dead of winter were often thought to portend the future. In the 16th century, for example, Germans cut boughs from fruit trees in November and took them into a warm room to grow. If many flowers bloomed by Christmas, the family would have good fortune in the coming year. Today, in similar fashion, we often force bulbs, such as amaryllis and paperwhites, to bloom uncharacteristically in December. Their fresh, bold blossoms are a cheerful addition to our festive decorations and a reminder of the promise of spring.

Flowers are a very welcome addition to the Christmas decorations in our homes. Their vibrant colors and sweet fragrances remind us that spring is just around the corner. Thanks to modern-day greenhouses and import florists, many varieties of fresh flowers are available, even in December. Dried and preserved flowers also offer a variety of decorating possibilities. These rosebud balls, made with miniature dried rosebuds, make delicate ornaments. Secure the rosebuds to a 2" (5 cm) Styrofoam® ball, following the instructions for a rosebud topiary on page 40; leave space for pinning and gluing a ribbon hanger in place.

Fragrant and exotic, fresh gardenias and seeded eucalyptus share the spotlight in this very formal and sweetly scented table wreath. The floral foam base, used in this arrangement and the one below, holds water to keep the flowers and greenery fresh for days.

Crimson, white, and green, the classic colors of Christmas, combine in brilliant contrasts to make this fresh and festive long-lasting centerpiece. The legendary poinsettias are native flowers of Mexico, introduced north of the border in 1828 by the first American ambassador to Mexico, Dr. Joel Poinsett. Their red color symbolizes atonement and sacrifice. The white of the carnations stands for purity and joy; the green branches for hope and life eternal.

A topiary is a classic floral arrangement. The size of topiaries can be varied, making them suitable for side tables, desks, or end tables. Group several topiaries of various sizes together for an eye-catching centerpiece on a mantel or buffet table.

For most topiaries, the base is a Styrofoam® ball secured to a branch or dowel and set into a pot with plaster of Paris. Make the base yourself, following the easy steps opposite. Or purchase a ready-made base at a floral or craft store; on some purchased bases, the ball is wire mesh instead of Styrofoam. Decorate the topiary with preserved boxwood, grapevine, dried rosebuds, dyed pistachios, or other embellishments, as shown opposite and on the following pages.

$\mathcal{H}$ow to make a Topiary

$\mathcal{M}$aterials

- Clay pot or ceramic vase.
- Self-adhesive felt, optional.
- Styrofoam ball.
- Branch or stained dowel for the trunk; additional twigs, if desired.
- Plaster of Paris; disposable container for mixing.
- Heavy-duty aluminum foil.
- Hot glue gun and glue sticks.
- Aerosol paint to match embellishments, if portions of the Styrofoam ball will be exposed between the embellishments.
- Saw, pruning shears, floral wire, and wire cutter may be needed for some projects, depending on materials selected.
- Spanish moss; embellishments as desired.

1 Line clay pot or vase with two layers of aluminum foil. Crumple foil loosely to shape of pot; edge of foil should be about ¾" (2 cm) below top of pot. If desired, affix self-adhesive felt circle to pot bottom.

2 Apply paint to Styrofoam ball, if desired. Insert trunk half-way into ball. Place trunk in pot; adjust height by cutting trunk to desired length. Remove the ball from the trunk.

3 Mix plaster of Paris, following the manufacturer's instructions. Pour plaster into pot, filling to foil edge. When plaster has started to thicken, insert trunk. Support the trunk using tape as shown, until plaster has set.

4 Apply hot glue into hole in Styrofoam ball; place ball on trunk. Conceal plaster with Spanish moss or items used to decorate tree. Embellish ball as desired.

2

3

4

39

Tiny dried rosebuds are delicate and elegant for small topiaries. For easier insertion of the rosebud stems, make holes in the painted Styrofoam® ball, using a toothpick, and dip the stems in craft glue before inserting them.

Dyed pistachios are used for casual topiaries that are inexpensive. On one small area at a time, apply hot glue to a painted Styrofoam ball and quickly secure the pistachios with the unopened end down.

Flowers and berries have appealing color and texture. The selections for the topiary are hydrangea florets and pepper berries.

Sheer French ribbon coils gently around this topiary. Rosebuds and other embellishments are either secured with hot glue or inserted directly into the ball.

Double topiaries are a variation of the basic style. A ready-made topiary base, purchased at a floral shop, was used for this large floor topiary. Pomegranates, oranges, and pinecones, secured with hot glue, are the primary embellishments.

Fruits are symbolic of the Christmas spirit, with an emphasis on generosity and hospitality. Holiday table decorations often include fresh fruits, such as apples, oranges, grapes, and pears. To extend the life of the decorations, artificial and dried fruits are useful for wreaths, garlands, and tree ornaments.

Sugared fruits and berries, laced with fresh sprigs of mint and rosemary create this stunning tiered centerpiece, perfect for a Christmas brunch. Two footed glass plates are stacked atop a larger glass plate and secured with floral putty. Fruits and berries are brushed with egg white, dipped in sugar, and placed in a balanced arrangement on the plates.

Artificial fruits and fresh boxwood, artfully arranged on a woodsy twig wreath brighten the view on a wintry day. All items are secured with hot glue. A wide ribbon, looped through the wreath and tied in a bow, provides a method for suspending the wreath in a window.

Streamers are made by wiring five strands of ribbon together, looping them at one end. Attach the wire to the top of the tree, letting the streamers fall freely, or tuck them lightly into the branches. The dried fruits may either be purchased or made, using a food dehydrator or oven.

43

How to make a Lemon Cone Tree

Tangy fresh lemons mingle with spicy cinnamon to create this fragrant, eye-appealing cone tree. Dried natural materials, such as statice, eucalyptus, and small pinecones offer contrasts in texture and color.

Materials

- Styrofoam® cone, about 18" (46 cm) high with 5" (12.5 cm) base.
- Woven basket with 5" (12.5 cm) base.
- Spanish moss.
- 18 to 20 small fresh lemons
- Statice and green eucalyptus, about 5 stems of each.
- 10 to 12 cinnamon sticks, 3" (7.5 cm) in length.
- 20 or more pinecones in various sizes; gold metallic aerosol paint.
- Decorative bird, optional.
- 4" (10 cm) wooden floral picks; 3" (7.5 cm) wooden floral picks with wire.
- 18-gauge wire; wire cutter.
- Hot glue gun and glue sticks.

1

1 Apply hot glue to the top of the inverted basket; secure cone to the basket. Puncture each fresh lemon at stem end with point of 4" (10 cm) wooden pick; insert flat end of pick into punctured lemon for about 2" (5 cm).

2 Secure lemons to the cone by inserting the picks, arranging lemons in a spiral around cone; wrap cone with a string to use as a guide. Arrange the Spanish moss around the lemons, pulling the moss apart so it loosely covers Styrofoam; secure with hot glue.
(continued)

$\mathcal{H}$ow to make a Lemon Cone Tree (continued)

3 Break the statice into small sprigs ranging from 2" to 6" (5 to 15 cm) long. Insert sprigs into cone, placing longer sprigs at bottom of cone and shorter sprigs toward top. Secure as necessary, using hot glue.

4 Attach a wooden pick with wire to the bottom of each pinecone by wrapping the wire around bottom layers of pinecone. Apply gold paint to the pinecones; for easier application, insert picks into a piece of Styrofoam. When dry, place the pinecones in the arrangement.

5 Attach 18-gauge wire to each cinnamon stick by inserting it through the length of the stick. Wrap the wire around the stick, twisting ends at the middle. Cut off one end of wire, using wire cutter; cut the other end to 2" or 3" (5 to 7.5 cm). Place wired cinnamon sticks in arrangement.

6 Cut eucalyptus into sprigs ranging from 3" to 4" (7.5 to 10 cm) long; break leaves off as necessary to make stem. Insert the sprigs, placing longer pieces at the bottom of the tree. Attach wooden pick to bird; insert near top of arrangement.

3

4

6

*H*ow to Oven-Dry *F*resh *F*ruit

Soak apple slices in one quart (0.9 L) water with two tablespoons (25 mL) lemon juice. Pat dry, using paper towel. Arrange ¼" (6 mm) slices of assorted fruits on baking sheet; separate slightly. Place in oven at 200ºF (95ºC); use exhaust fan to remove humidity as fruit dries. Bake about two hours; timing varies with fleshiness and quantity of fruit. Remove when fruit is leathery.

47

Seashells

Even in landlocked European countries, seashells have long been symbolic of eternal life, resurrection, and transformation. In Roman and Greek mythology, the scallop shell was the symbol of Venus or Aphrodite, the goddess of love and beauty, who was believed to have risen in birth from the sea. In her honor, ancient Greeks wore stylized scallop shells as shoulder clasps for their tunics. Early Christians adopted the scallop as a religious symbol, some say because Jesus's Apostles were fishermen. In Britain, the scallop shell appears in the coat of arms for families who's Catholic ancestors had participated in the Crusades.

The sea star, of course, reminds us of the Bethlehem star that led the Wise Men. Distinctive markings on the common sand dollar, including the center star and a poinsettia, have inspired poems to be written, attributing it Christmas symbolism. When broken open, this shell releases five white doves to spread good will and peace.

How to make a Seashell Snowflake Ornament

Purchase the sliced and lily-cut conical shells for this ornament at nature shops or specialty shell stores.

Materials

- 5" (12.5 cm) ribbon, ¼" (6 mm) wide, in desired color.
- 1" (2.5 cm) diameter plastic, wood, or tagboard, disk.
- Six center-cut slices of equal length from chula or strawberry strombus seashells, for outer layer.
- Six lily-cut shells of equal length from chula or strawberry seashells, for inner layer.
- One umbonium or snail shell, ¼" to ½" (6 mm to 1.3 cm) diameter, for center.
- Craft glue.

1 Lap ribbon ends to form loop; glue to disk, and allow to dry. Arrange chula slices side by side. Note curves and spaces; turn slices over as necessary so all longest spaces are on the same side.

2 Place ⅛" (3 mm) glue dot on underside of chula slice, at narrow tip. Lap about ½" (1.3 cm) of slice onto disk. Repeat quickly with remaining slices. Adjust lap amount so slices are evenly spaced on an imaginary circle. Allow to dry several hours.

3 Place ⅛" (3 mm) glue dot on lily-cut shell back, ¼" (6 mm) from narrow tip. Place tip over disk center so shell back rests between two slices and curled lip is on the top. Repeat quickly with remaining lily-cut shells; adjust so cut tops are evenly spaced on an imaginary circle. Glue umbonium shell at center to hide tips. Allow to dry overnight.

1

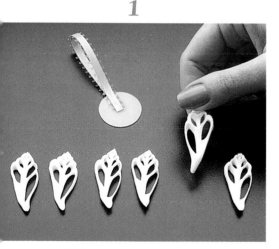

2

3

50

How to make a Seashell Angel Ornament

Materials

- ⅜" to ⅝" (1 to 1.5 cm) wood bead, for head; acrylic paints and fine-tip brush.
- 10" (25.5 cm) 8-lb. (3.5 kg) monofilament fishing line, for hanger.
- Craft glue; mat knife.
- Miniature shells, for hair.
- Round seashell, larger than head, for halo.
- Large attractive shell, for gown.
- Ribbon, felt, suede, or Ultrasuede® strip, ¼" to ½" (6 mm to 1.3 cm) wide, for wings; scissors.
- Embellishments as desired.

1 Paint eyes and mouth on head. Knot ends of hanger to form loop; secure to bead hole or back of head, using glue. Glue miniature shells to top and sides of head, for hair, bringing hair close to face to prevent appearance of baldness; leave back of head bare.

2 Apply glue to halo hinge. Place gown hinge over halo, lapping shells about ⅛" (3 mm). Secure head to halo bowl and snug against body, using glue. Allow to dry thoroughly; check shells occasionally to make sure they remain snug.

3 Cut wing strip equal in length to four times body height. Place glue drop at strip center; turn strip onto glue at slight diagonal to form loop that is slightly more than half the body width. Repeat to form second loop.

4 Apply glue along upper edge and hinge of gown; secure wings. Trim ends diagonally, pointing away from gown. Embellish as desired. Trim any visible glue from ornament with mat knife.

1

2

3

Spices

Throughout history, the richest, most powerful country in the world has been the one that controlled the spice trade. In ancient times, the extravagant use of spices for seasonings, preservatives, medicines, personal indulgences, and ceremonial incense was reserved only for the wealthy. So coveted were the aromas, tastes, and healing powers of spices, that the quest for control of the lands where spices were grown led to the exploration and discovery of the modern world. Though today we take for granted the abundance and easy accessibility of all kinds of spices, they held a prestigious roll in early Christmas celebrations. Just as the gifts of the Magi included exotic spices from the East, families honored the Christmas season with delicacies enriched by spices like cinnamon, ginger, cloves, or nutmeg. Nothing conjures up the Christmas spirit like the heady aroma of these spices wafting from the kitchen.

How to make a Spice Ornament

Spice ornaments are fragrant and colorful additions to the holiday tree. They are made by covering Styrofoam® balls with powdered or crushed dried spices. To create a variety of looks, the simple ornaments can be embellished with ribbons and preserved or artificial leaves or berries. For durability, the spice-covered ornaments are sprayed with an aerosol clear acrylic sealer.

Materials

- Powdered or crushed dried spices, such as nutmeg, cinnamon, oregano, mace, paprika, parsley, poppy seed, crushed red pepper, allspice, mustard seed, chili powder, or dried orange peel.
- Aerosol acrylic paints in colors that blend with spices.
- Styrofoam balls.
- 20-gauge craft wire.
- 9" (23 cm) length of ribbon or cording, for hanger.
- Thick craft glue; hot glue gun and glue sticks.
- Aerosol clear acrylic sealer.
- Embellishments as desired.

1 Roll Styrofoam ball lightly against table to compress the Styrofoam slightly.

2 Spray Styrofoam ball with aerosol acrylic paint; allow to dry.

3 Apply craft glue to the Styrofoam ball; roll in spice to cover. Allow to dry. Apply aerosol acrylic sealer.

4 Knot the ends of the ribbon or cording together. Bend 4" (10 cm) length of wire in half. Attach ribbon or cording to the ornament with wire as shown; secure with dot of hot glue.

5 Secure any additional embellishments to the ornament as desired, using hot glue.

3

4

5

How to make a Cinnamon Star Tree Topper

Cinnamon, derived from the aromatic bark of certain tropical Asian trees, is an essential Christmas spice. Dried, curled sticks of cinnamon bark are used to make this primitive five-pointed star to place atop the Christmas tree.

1 Arrange two cinnamon sticks in an X; position a third stick across the top, placing one end below upper stick of X as shown.

2 Place remaining two sticks on top in an inverted V. Adjust spacing of cinnamon sticks as necessary, to form star. Secure sticks at ends, using hot glue.

3 Tie raffia securely around ends at intersection of cinnamon sticks. Tie several lengths of raffia into bow; glue to top of star. Secure embellishments with glue.

Materials

- Five 12" (30.5 cm) cinnamon sticks.
- Hot glue gun and glue sticks.
- Raffia.
- Embellishments, such as cones and sprigs of greenery.

1

2

3

How to make a Cinnamon-Stick Bundle

Bundles of cinnamon sticks, glued together and tied with ribbon, make quick, fragrant ornaments. Embellish with a sprig of greenery.

Materials

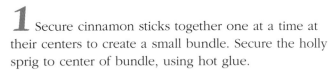

- Several long cinnamon sticks.
- Artificial holly sprig.
- Ribbon or raffia, for hanger.
- Hot glue gun and glue sticks.

1

1 Secure cinnamon sticks together one at a time at their centers to create a small bundle. Secure the holly sprig to center of bundle, using hot glue.

2 Tie ribbon around center of bundle to conceal any hot glue drops. Tie loop at center of ornament for hanger.

Seeds & Grains

When man first realized that the seeds of a plant could sprout and grow into new plants, his naive interpretation of this phenomenon led him to believe that seeds had magical powers. As centuries passed and people acquired the knowledge and sophistication to grow plants for food, their reverence and respect for seeds and grains remained, for in them was held the promise for the future and a new beginning. Early Christians naturally adopted the seed as a symbol of their faith. So precious were seeds and grains, that to share them with other people or animals was to actually share life with them. European Christmas customs included showing extra kindness to animals. Such kindnesses were believed to bring prosperity to the givers in the new year. Scandinavian immigrants to America customarily provided wheat for birds, tying sheaves of grain atop poles or in trees, while German immigrants decorated outdoor trees with fruits, nuts, and breads.

How to build a Grain Stand

Birds gather at grain sources; they like regular and bearded wheat, oats, barley, millet, sorghum, and foxtail. Miniature corn and dried sunflowers are other favorites, and many birds love raw peanuts. Seeds may be pressed into a layer of peanut butter spread over cones. Breads and popcorn should be avoided; they are filling and don't provide sufficient energy. Suet is a favorite attraction because it provides long-lasting, warming energy. Assorted berries, such as cranberries, holly, bittersweet, rose hips, and red pepperberries, provide colorful embellishments as well as food; avoid using dyed naturals or imitations. Small fresh fruits, such as crabapples and kumquats, are sweet treats. Dried fruit slices may be purchased or dried at home in a dehydrator or oven (page 47). Small cones, colorful peppers, and a variety of pods, such as lotus and poppy, may be added for interest.

Materials

- Container, such as wooden tote, window box, terra-cotta pot, or urn.
- Sand to fill container; paper.
- Grain stalks; string.
- Birdseed as desired.
- Embellishments as desired.

1 Measure container depth. Trim grain stalks so total length is no more than five times container depth; tie bundles near the center.

2 Line container with paper; partially fill container with sand. Push bundles to container bottom; add more sand, and top with birdseed to container rim. Embellish container as desired.

1

2

How to build a Suet House

Materials

- Rough-sawn 1 × 8 cedar or redwood; saw.
- Drill; drill bits in assorted sizes.
- Four galvanized screws, 1½" (3.8 cm) long.
- ½" (1.3 cm) hardware cloth, cut into two 6" × 4½" (15 × 11.5 cm) pieces; staple gun.
- 1 yd. (0.95 m) heavy leather lacing or polyurethane cord; two screw eyes.
- Embellishments as desired; string or raffia.
- Suet block, about 4½" × 4½" × 1½" (11.5 × 11.5 × 3.8 cm).

1 Saw wood into these pieces: 8" (20.5 cm) square base, 8" × 5" (20.5 × 12.5 cm) roof, two 1¾" × 5" (4.5 × 12.5 cm) uprights. Drill ⅛" (3 mm) hole ½" (1.3 cm) from edge, at center of each short side of base. Repeat on roof. Drill two ⅛" (3 mm) holes on each short side of base, drilling each hole ½" (1.3 cm) from center and 1⅛" (2.8 cm) from edge. Drill two ⅛" (3 mm) holes on center line of one upright end, 1" (2.5 cm) apart; repeat on other upright. Secure uprights to base, inserting screws through small holes from underside of base.

2 Secure hardware cloth to upright sides, using staples. Drill hole on outside of each upright, ⅜" (1 cm) from top; insert screw eyes. Knot lacing end. Slip lacing from base bottom through screw eye, roof holes, opposite screw eye, and return to base bottom; knot loose end. Tie knot near lacing center to form 3" (7.5 cm) loop, for hanger. Insert suet into holder; tie other edibles to screw eyes, using string or raffia.

1

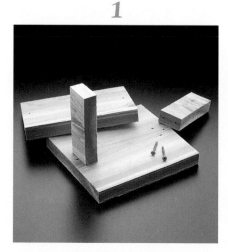

2

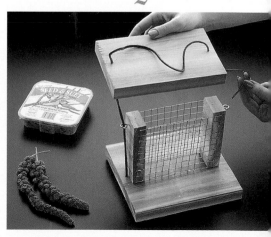